SURVIVAL SKILLS HANDBOOK

MAPS AND
NAVIGATION

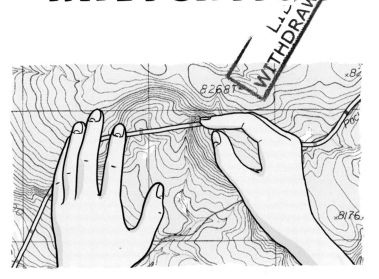

Bear Grylls

This survival handbook has been specially put together to help young adventurers just like you to stay safe in the wild. Learning essential skills such as map reading and navigation will allow you to truly experience the world around you. Although it requires practice and practical application, there is nothing like the sense of achievement you will feel upon successfully finding your way to your planned destination!

Bear

CONTENTS

STARTING YOUR ADVENTURE

The world is full of exciting places to explore. In order to stay safe on your travels you will need to learn the art of navigation and map reading, like the adventurers of the past. As long as you have a map and compass, and know how to use them, you need never get lost. Remember, practice makes perfect!

Equipment

If you venture into the wild, make sure you have all the equipment you need so that you can get from one place to another as quickly and easily as possible. The type of equipment and the amount you need depends upon where you are going and for how long. Here are some of the basics you will need when going walking.

thermal hat or sun hat, depending on the weather

waterproof jacket in case of rain

layers of clothing so you can add more if it is cold, or take some off if you are too warm

rucksack

watch

warm gloves

sensible trousers, such as walking trousers

sensible footwear such as walking boots and thick socks

Make sure you carry these essentials in your rucksack or day bag.

compass

map

first-aid kit

food and bottle of water

torch

mobile phone

camera

sunscreen and insect repellant

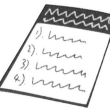

emergency contact details

BEAR SAYS

Make sure someone knows your route and estimated arrival time before you set off so they can raise the alarm if you don't turn up when expected.

MAPS

Map care

As you walk, you will need to look at your map quite often to check you are on the right track. Maps need to be folded carefully to keep them in good condition so that they stay useful.

A map case with a neck cord may be a good idea, while some outdoor clothing has a specially designed large map pocket – if you are keeping the map in a bag, make sure it is easily accessible when you are out. Laminated maps can be useful if you are likely to be outside in wet or windy weather conditions. A spare may also be essential if you are somewhere remote.

How to fold a map

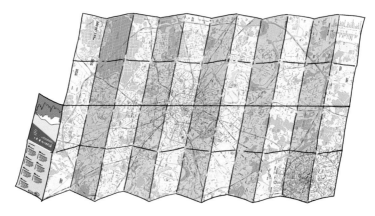

1 Although it sounds easy, folding a map can be tricky. With your map spread open, look at the creases – they should show the correct places to fold.

2 Fold the map in half by bringing the top edge to meet the bottom edge.

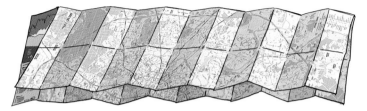

make sure the cover is out to one side

3 Fold the map inwards, as though it is an accordion.

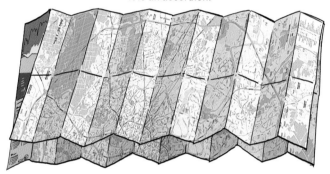

4 Fold the map over so that the cover is on top. Some maps have a third section that needs to be tucked in.

✖

BEAR SAYS

Explorers should be good at drawing maps, so it is important to get lots of practice. You never know when you might need these skills!

Topographical maps

These maps show contour lines and landforms. They are useful because they show how the ground is shaped. Every hiker should be able to "read" the contour lines on the map so that they can plan their route.

Contour lines

Each contour line on a map joins up points where the ground is the same height. Lines close together mean that there is a steep slope, while lines that are far apart indicate flat ground or a gentle slope.

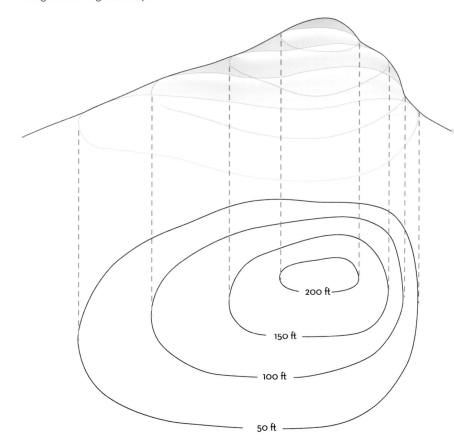

200 ft

150 ft

100 ft

50 ft

Choosing the best route

The best route to a destination may not be the most direct. Choose a path that is safe – for example on footpaths – and stay away from any hazards like cliffs and fast-moving water. Make it as simple as possible so that it is easy to follow and make sure you have permission to be on the land if it isn't a public right of way.

Landmark spotting

From your known start point, look for the nearest and biggest landmark on your map, such as a lake. Check the contour lines in case it is hidden from view. If you don't know where you are, mark any notable landmarks around you on a piece of paper and then see if you can match them up to your map. The scale may be tricky to guess but it is good start if you are unsure of your location.

BEAR SAYS

Understanding contour lines and being able to visualize your environment from a map is a great skill to have under your belt.

NORTH

WEST

EAST

SOUTH

How to measure distance

Map measurers allow you to find the distances between two points on a map. Route planning is an important part of navigation, and knowing how far you need to travel will help you work out your finish time – and if you'll arrive before dark!

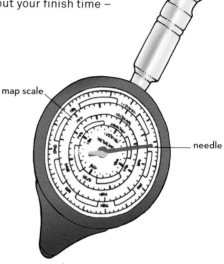

map scale

needle

Analogue map reader

This tool uses a needle and dial printed with different map scales to show distance in miles or kilometres.

Using your compass

As well as taking bearings and helping you find north, your orienteering compass can help you find distances, using the measurements on the base plate.

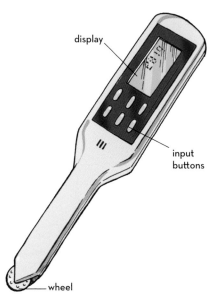

display

input buttons

wheel

Digital map reader

With digital map reader wheels, the user sets the unit, such as kilometres, and the map scale. They then run the tip of the reader along the route to find the distance.

⋀

BEAR SAYS

Measuring distance accurately will help you plan your hike. Take the time to take measurements before you set off.

Using a piece of string

If you are without a device, you can place a piece of string along your route, and then along the distance scale on the map.

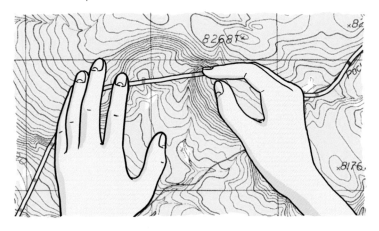

Types of landscape

As you walk around the countryside you will notice that there are many different types of landscape. Some are far easier to travel along than others. These are some of the most common types.

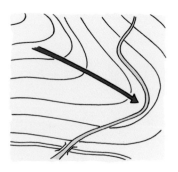 

Gentle slope

This slope decreases steadily in height and makes for an easy climb.

Steep slope

Steep slopes are hard to trek up, due to the sharp angle of the land.

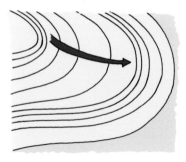

Concave slope

This kind of slope is steep at the top but less so at the bottom, a little like the curve inside a bowl.

BEAR SAYS

Make sure you avoid steep climbs! A knowledge of contour lines will help you pick the best paths while navigating.

Convex slope

A rounded slope that goes from less steep to steep.

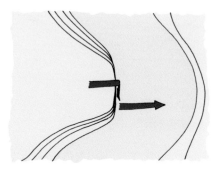

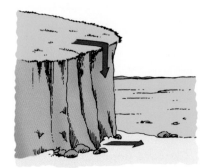

Cliff

A cliff is a very steep drop in the landscape, often at coasts.

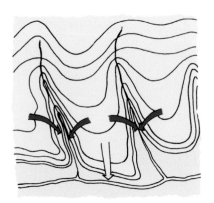

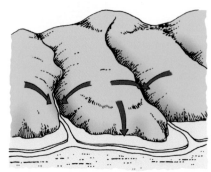

Gullies and spurs

Gullies are steep ravines found close to the seashore, while spurs are the ridges of land that slope down from the edge of a hill.

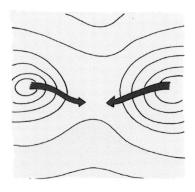

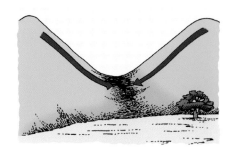

Saddle

The area between two connecting hills or mountain peaks is called a saddle.

BEAR SAYS

A landscape is made up of different geographic features that can be used make navigation much easier.

Valley

A valley is a low area of land found between hills. Rivers are often found in valleys.

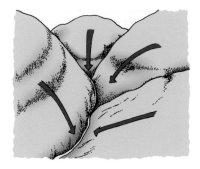

Symbols

Maps use symbols, lines, and colours to describe what is on the land and make the map clearer.

Learn the pictures

If you look closely at a map you can see it is covered in symbols. It would be almost impossible to write everything out in words on a map – there just isn't enough space. A key (or legend) explains what these symbols mean. The symbols could be pictures, words, or abbreviations.

A symbol for Mars

Ordnance Survey is the national mapping agency for Great Britain and is one of the world's largest producers of maps. The symbols used on these maps are easily recognizable and in May 2016 they held a competition to design a symbol for Mars as it has been recently mapped.

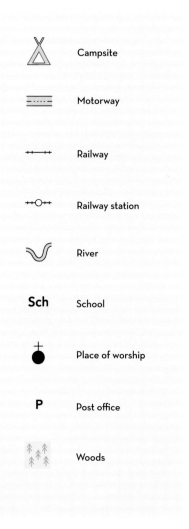

Campsite

Motorway

Railway

Railway station

River

Sch   School

Place of worship

P   Post office

Woods

Scales

Maps are made to scale so that the distance between landmarks and places in real life is shown accurately on paper. It is very important that the map is correct, so that features are where the map reader expects. Scale also helps us to work out distances. Most maps have a scale written on them (e.g. 1:50,000). This means that one centimetre on the map represents 50,000 cm on the ground.

Small scale

The scale is shown visually on a map in both centimetres and inches. In this example, this diagram shows a map with a scale of 1:100,000. In this case every one centimetre on the map is equal to one kilometre on the ground.

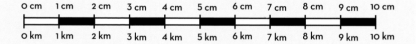

BEAR SAYS

Learning the symbols can take time at first but they are quite straightforward. Put the time in to make sure you recognize them now to make life easier.

Coordinates

Coordinates can describe any location on Earth. Our planet is a globe or sphere, and around it are a set of imaginary rings drawn from east to west and north to south. The lines running from the top to the bottom of the globe are called lines of longitude, while the lines running around it are called lines of latitude.

Lines of latitude

Latitude is measured in degrees north or south of the equator (0–90°). The equator is an imaginary line that runs round the centre of the planet, and is itself a line of latitude. It divides the Earth into two parts – the northern and southern hemispheres.

Lines of longitude

Lines of longitude run around the Earth from north to south. They are called meridians. Longitude is measured in degrees east or west of the Greenwich meridian (0–180°).

northern hemisphere

WEST

equator

SOUTH

BEAR SAYS

Using longitude and latitude you can accurately describe any location on Earth.

Where do you live?

The coordinate system can be used to pinpoint anywhere on the planet, and works in any language because it relies on numbers. You can look up the latitude and longitude of where you live on the internet.

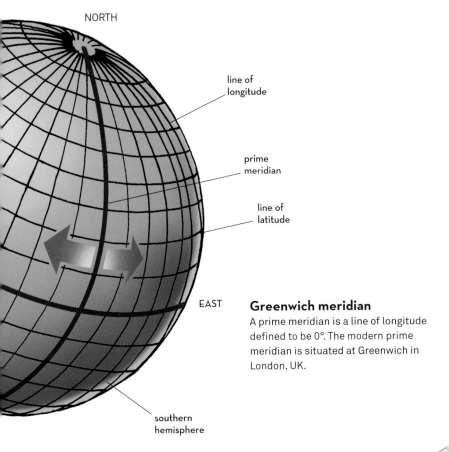

NORTH

line of longitude

prime meridian

line of latitude

EAST

southern hemisphere

Greenwich meridian

A prime meridian is a line of longitude defined to be 0°. The modern prime meridian is situated at Greenwich in London, UK.

From globe to map

Our planet is a sphere – but maps are flat. In order to create a map, cartographers have to "project" the 3D globe onto 2D paper by squashing and stretching it. Luckily, the changes made to the globe are too small to cause big problems on most hiking maps.

EARTH

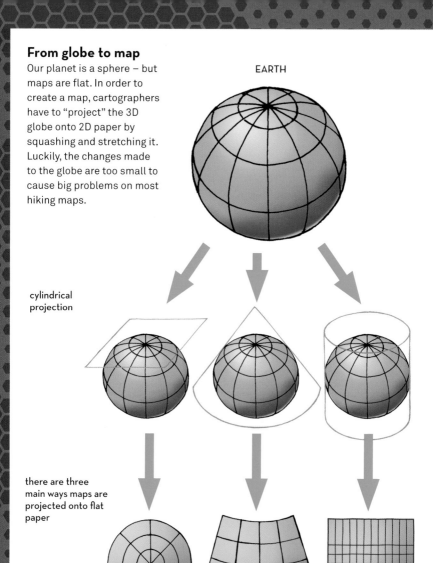

cylindrical projection

there are three main ways maps are projected onto flat paper

Grid references

Maps are often divided into squares called grids. These grids help to pinpoint a location on the map quickly. The vertical lines crossing the map from top to bottom are called "eastings" because the numbers go up as you move east across the map. The horizontal lines crossing the map from one side to the other are called "northings" as the numbers increase as you get further north.

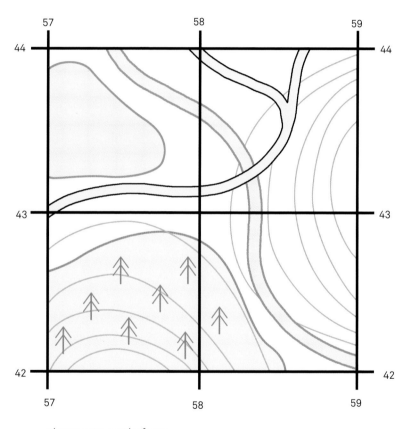

when you give a grid reference you always give the easting first.
The forest is in 4257

MAGNETIC EARTH

Our planet is one big magnet, which is very useful for navigation – just as long as you have a map, a compass, and an understanding of how magnetic north and true north differ.

Earth's magnetic field

At Earth's centre is liquid iron. This metal core makes our planet into a giant magnet, with a magnetic field that changes over time. Because magnetic north is not at the geographic North Pole, you need to make special adjustments when using a compass. This is known as declination.

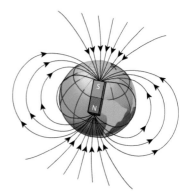

Earth's magnetic field is strongest near the North and South Poles.

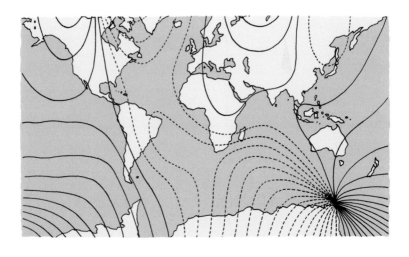

Which way is north?

When we talk about "true north" we mean the top of Earth – the geographic North Pole. Earth spins around, and if you imagine it is spinning around a line that goes from the top to the bottom of the planet, the North Pole is the point at the very top, and the South Pole is the point at the very bottom. Magnetic north is different as it responds to Earth's changing magnetic field, and doesn't line up with the same point.

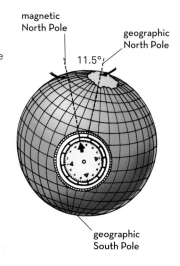

magnetic
North Pole

geographic
North Pole

11.5°

geographic
South Pole

Three norths

Good maps will have a key to indicate grid, true (geographic), and magnetic north.

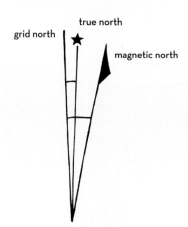

grid north

true north

magnetic north

BEAR SAYS

GPS systems are not affected by the earth's magnetic field, so they can be a useful piece of kit, especially in the far north.

COMPASSES

The compass was invented in China around a thousand years ago and it is still used today by navigators needing to find their direction of travel. It works using a tiny magnet controlled by Earth's magnetic field, which makes the compass point north.

Which compass should I use?

An orienteering compass is a great place to start. It has a transparent base and is designed to be used with a topographical map. It is is a very useful piece of kit and, with practice, is easy to use. No matter which way you turn, the magnetic needle always points north, so you can discover which way is north, east, south, and west.

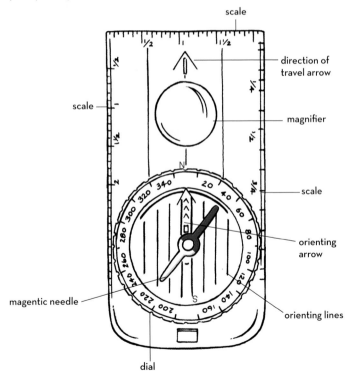

scale

direction of travel arrow

scale

magnifier

scale

orienting arrow

magentic needle

orienting lines

dial

Orient a map

To orient a map you need to align the edge of your compass with the north–south lines of your map. Set the dial of your compass to north, then turn the map and compass together until the north (red) end of the compass needle is directly over the orienting arrow. Your map is now correctly oriented.

when the map is correctly oriented, a line drawn from your position on the map to a mapped landmark will point to the actual landmark

to true north

to true north

your location on map

Take a bearing

The angle between north and an object is called a bearing. They are measured in degrees, for example 45 degrees (45°). Bearings are always measured clockwise – you start facing north and turn to the right until you reach the angle of the bearing. Then you should be facing your destination. A bearing can also be known as a "magnetic" or "true" bearing depending upon whether it is measured from true north or magnetic north.

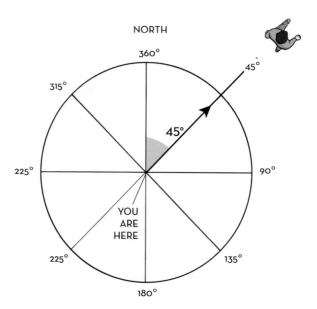

NORTH

360°

315°

45°

45°

225°

90°

YOU
ARE
HERE

225°

135°

180°

Try it yourself!

These diagrams show a hiker walking in three different directions. Can you work out his bearing for each picture?

BEAR SAYS

Also double check your bearings! If you start out in even slightly the wrong direction you could add hours to your trek.

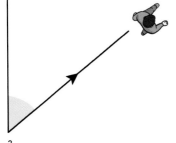

1

3

2

290° .3 50° .2 5° .1

Answers

27

Get your bearing

1 First align the desired bearing on the dial with the direction of travel arrow.

2 Hold the compass in front of you and turn your body until the north end of the compass needle is directly over the orienting arrow.

head this way

Taking a bearing from a map

Your map does not have to be oriented to take a bearing. Place the compass on the map with the edge lined up against your desired line of travel. Rotate the dial until the "N" is aligned with the top of the map and the orienting lines are parallel with the north–south lines on the map. The bearing on the dial is the bearing you should follow.

92   93   94   95   96

Bypassing objects

You can also use bearings to make your way around obstacles.

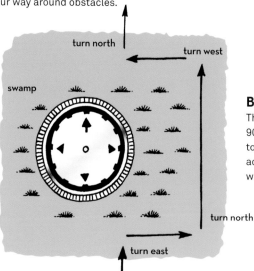

turn north

turn west

swamp

turn north

turn east

Basic bypass

This bypass involves three 90-degree turns with a fourth to bring you back on track. For accuracy, count your paces when bypassing.

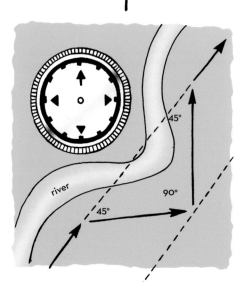

45°

river

90°

45°

45- and 90-degree bypass

This bypass involves just three turns. Count your paces to ensure that each length is of equal distance.

Marker

Bypassing is easy if you can see a feature beyond the obstacle aligned with your bearing. In this case, walk around the lake until you reach the lone tree.

BEAR SAYS

Learning how to make bypasses to avoid dangerous obstacles can save precious time on a hike that could be spent setting up camp or preparing food.

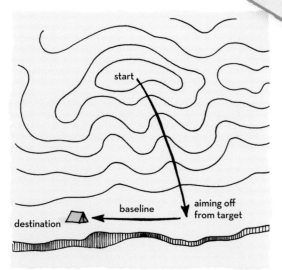

Deliberate offset

Take a bearing left or right of your destination. That way, when you hit a "baseline", such as a road or river, you know which way to turn.

Other types of compass

Mirror sighting compass

This compass type is similar to an orienteering compass with the addition of a hinged mirror. This allows you to sight your target and your bearing at the same time.

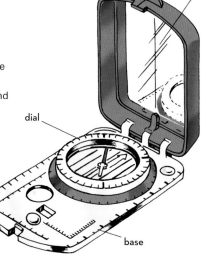

mirror

dial

base

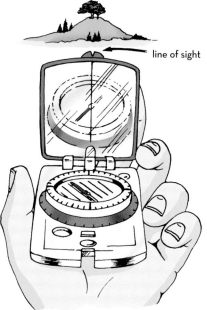

line of sight

BEAR SAYS

Trying out different compasses is not only useful, but fun too. Each has its own benefits.

Lensatic compass

In situations when an exact reading is required, a lensatic compass is best. They are the favoured compass type for military use. Many models have illuminated dial markings so they can be used at night.

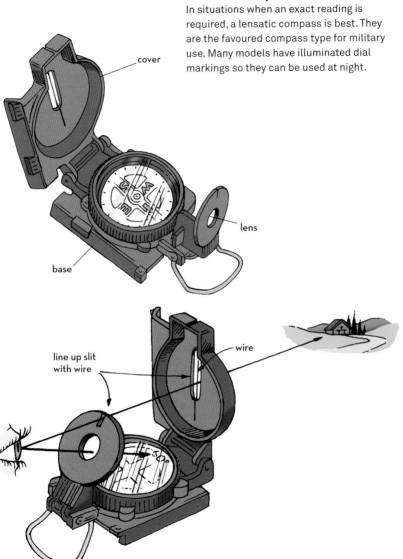

cover

lens

base

line up slit with wire

wire

Thumb compass
These thumb-mounted compasses are used in orienteering.

Direct sighting
Look through the eyepiece to get a bearing accurate to within one degree.

Button
A compass doesn't have to be big to be useful. Keep a little one in reserve.

BEAR SAYS
Some mobile phones even come with a compass! You can't rely on the battery life though – so they aren't a replacement for proper kit.

Make your own compass

These are some simple ways to make your own magnetic device.

Magnetize

To make a compass, first magnetize a needle by stroking it in one direction with a magnet. If you stroke towards the point of your needle, the point will indicate north.

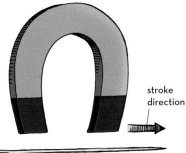

stroke direction

needle

insulated wire

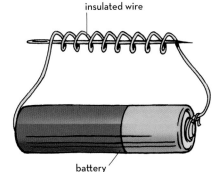

Battery method

Alternatively, you can magnetize a needle by coiling some insulated wire around it. Connect the wire to a battery for five to ten minutes.

battery

mug

Now you know

If you gently lower the needle into a mug of water, surface tension should keep it floating (a coating of natural oil from your hair will help). The sharp end will point towards magnetic north.

GPS

Hand-held GPS units are a fantastic aid to navigation, and can be the difference between life and death in extreme survival conditions. However, they can't replace maps – you should always carry a compass and know how to use it in case your equipment fails.

The global positioning system

A GPS unit works by measuring its exact distance from a minimum of three satellites in space. The point at which the three signals intersect is shown with a black dot below. This point represents the position of the GPS unit on Earth.

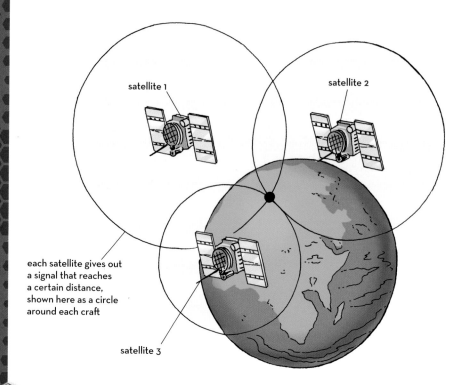

satellite 1

satellite 2

each satellite gives out a signal that reaches a certain distance, shown here as a circle around each craft

satellite 3

Go on a treasure hunt

If you like exploring, and have a GPS device, you can join the many hundreds of people who enjoy "geocaching". This hobby involves navigating to a set of coordinates and finding a container (the geocache) that has been hidden at that particular spot.

BEAR SAYS

There are 24 satellites in space that work together to make an accurate view of Earth.

Hand-held unit

A hand-held GPS unit will tell you your location, speed, and approximate altitude (height above sea or ground level). It will also permit you to retrace your path, guide you to specific waypoints or landmarks, and will work as a compass as long as you are moving in one direction. The more expensive models come with built-in maps, electronic compasses, and barometers (devices that measure pressure in the atmosphere).

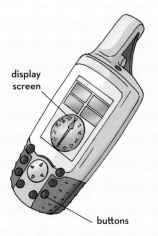

display screen

buttons

OTHER WAYS TO NAVIGATE

Even without a compass it is possible to determine direction. The sun, moon, and stars can be signposts if you know how to read them. There are also lots of clues in the living world that can help you find your way.

Navigating the night sky

Looking up at the starry night sky is beautiful – and it can be useful too. The North and South Celestial Poles are the points in the night sky that appear to be directly overhead at all times. Finding these points can help you find the right directions. To find the north polar star (Polaris), first locate the pattern of stars known as the Plough or Big Dipper (Ursa Major). To find the south polar star, first find the constellation Crux.

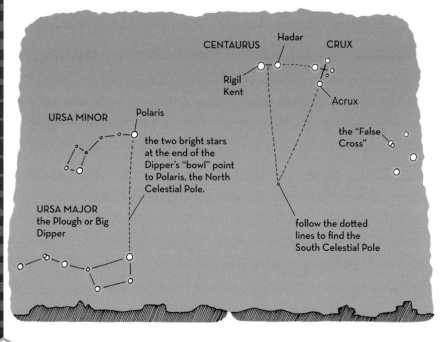

CENTAURUS Hadar CRUX

Rigil Kent

Acrux

URSA MINOR Polaris

the two bright stars at the end of the Dipper's "bowl" point to Polaris, the North Celestial Pole.

the "False Cross"

URSA MAJOR
the Plough or Big Dipper

follow the dotted lines to find the South Celestial Pole

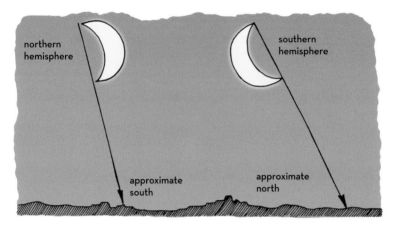

Lunar method

Imagine a line connecting the "horns" of the crescent Moon and project it to the horizon. This point indicates approximate south in the northern hemisphere or north in the southern hemisphere.

northern hemisphere

southern hemisphere

approximate south

approximate north

Watch method

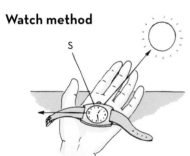

S

N

Northern hemisphere

Point the hour hand at the Sun. Divide the angle between the hour hand and the 12 mark in half to find south.

Southern hemisphere

Point the 12 mark at the Sun. Divide the angle between the hour hand and the 12 mark in half to find north.

Shadow tip method

The shadow tip method works in either hemisphere and is most accurate around noon.

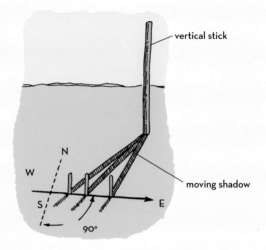

vertical stick

moving shadow

1 Firstly, place a stick vertically in the ground. Mark the tip of the shadow made by the stick with a pebble or another stick.

2 Wait at least ten minutes before marking the shadow's tip with a second marker.

3 As the sun sets in the west the marks will move east. Join the marks to create a line that runs from west to east. Draw another line straight through the east-west line at a 90-degree angle. This will indicate north.

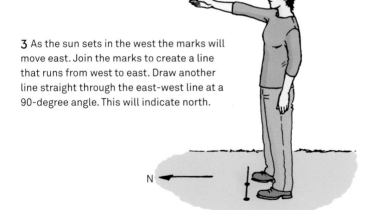

Compass-free map method

Align the features on a map with the corresponding features in the landscape. This will allow you to determine direction and work out your position.

point B on the map (a hill) lines up with point B in the landscape

point A (a church) on the map lines up with point A in the landscape

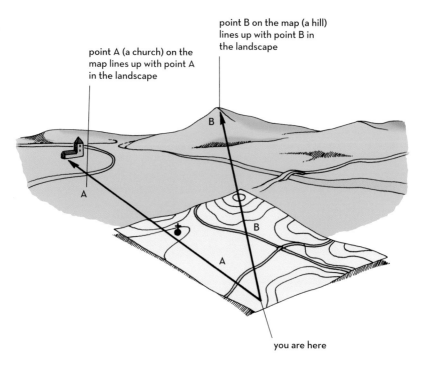

you are here

Night star method

This simple method uses stars to pinpoint your location.

1 Set a long stick into the ground at a slight angle. Tie a length of string to the end of the stick. Lie on your back, place the string by your temple, and align it with a well-known star.

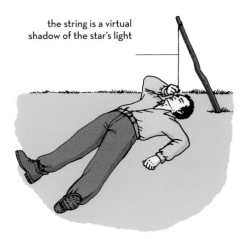

the string is a virtual shadow of the star's light

2 Mark the star's position on the ground and then wait a while before marking it for a second time. As with the shadow tip method, the first mark will be west and the second will be east.

mark the position with a stick

Signs in nature

Snow
Melted snow on one side of a tree will indicate south in the northern hemisphere.

Glacial boulders
These large rocks sit on pedestals of ice that erode on the south side in the northern hemisphere.

Green sign
Moss usually grows better on the shady side of a tree trunk – that's the north side in the northern hemisphere.

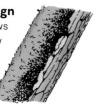

Magnetic termites
These Australian termites build their mounds aligned north–south to minimize exposure to the sun.

Traveller's palm
The leaves of this palm form a dramatic fan that is usually aligned east–west.

Nesting birds
If you are near water, look for signs of breeding wildlife, e.g. nests or frogspawn. Water birds, fish, and frogs often breed on the west side of a river or lake.

Prevailing wind

The most common wind direction that a location experiences is called the prevailing wind. The place the wind has come from brings different types of weather. The prevailing south-west wind in Britain, for example, is partly why it often rains more than other countries.

Spider webs

Do you know which way the wind tends to blow? Spiders do, and will orient their webs sideways to the prevailing wind.

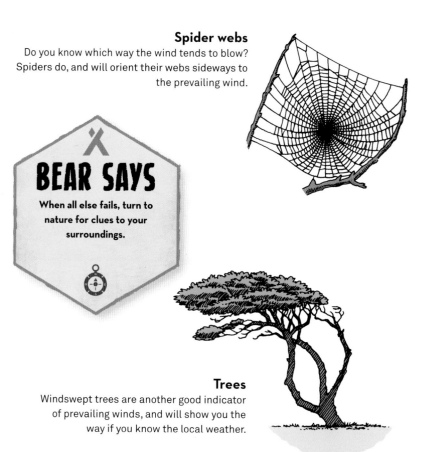

BEAR SAYS

When all else fails, turn to nature for clues to your surroundings.

Trees

Windswept trees are another good indicator of prevailing winds, and will show you the way if you know the local weather.

GLOSSARY

Analogue An analogue device usually has a needle or pointer (think about clocks) and can show a continuously variable number.

Bearing A bearing is the angle measured between north and an actual object.

Bypass A bypass is an alternative route around an object.

Compass An instrument used for finding your way, often alongside a map.

Concave Curving in or hollowed inward.

Contour A line that shows the 3D shape of something.

Convex A convex shape is curved or rounded outwards.

Coordinates A system that means every location on Earth can be described by a set of numbers.

Digital A digital device usually has a computerized display.

Kilometre A unit of length equal to one thousand metres.

Landmark An object that is easily seen from a distance.

Orienteering A sport involving navigational skills using a map and compass.

Prevailing wind The most frequent wind direction experienced at a particular location.

Scale The relationship between the distance on a map to the corresponding distance on the ground.

Symbol A picture, word, or abbreviation on a map.

Termite An insect that usually lives in a large group.

Topographical A topographical map shows the shape of the ground (e.g. flat or hilly) using contour lines.

Discover more amazing books in the Bear Grylls series:

Perfect for young adventurers, the *Survival Skills* series accompanies an exciting range of colouring and activity books. Curious kids can also learn tips and tricks for almost any extreme situation in *Survival Camp*, and explore Earth in *Extreme Planet*.

Conceived by Weldon Owen in partnership with Bear Grylls Ventures

Produced by Weldon Owen Ltd
Suite 3.08 The Plaza, 535 King's Road,
London SW10 0SZ, UK

WELDON OWEN LTD
Publisher Donna Gregory
Designer Shahid Mahmood
Editorial Claire Philip, Sophia Podini
Illustrators Peter Bull Studios (original illustrations),
Bernard Chau (colour)

Printed in Malaysia

10 9 8 7 6 5 4 3 2 1

Disclaimer
Weldon Owen and Bear Grylls take pride in doing our best to get the facts right in putting together the information in this book, but occasionally something slips past our beady eyes. Therefore we make no warranties about the accuracy or completeness of the information in the book and to the maximum extent permitted, we disclaim all liability. Wherever possible, we will endeavour to correct any errors of fact at reprint.

Kids – if you want to try any of the activities in this book, please ask your parents first! Parents – all outdoor activities carry some degree of risk and we recommend that anyone participating in these activities be aware of the risks involved and seek professional instruction and guidance. None of the health/medical information in this book is intended as a substitute for professional medical advice; always seek the advice of a qualified practitioner.

A WELDON OWEN PRODUCTION.
PART OF THE BONNIER PUBLISHING GROUP.